AMERICA
OPEN YOUR GIFT.

---

119 MILLION NEW MILLIONAIRES

MAKE AME RICA GREAT AGAIN
HANDRI TIMBULENG

AMERICA OPEN YOUR GIFT.

This book is written to provide information and motivation to readers. Its purpose is not to render any type of psychological, legal, or professional advice of any kind. The content is the sole opinion and expression of the author, and not necessarily that of the publisher.

Copyright © 2019 by HANDRI TIMBULENG

All rights reserved. No part of this book may be reproduced, transmitted, or distributed in any form by any means, including, but not limited to, recording, photocopying, or taking screenshots of parts of the book, without prior written permission from the author or the publisher. Brief quotations for noncommercial purposes, such as book reviews, permitted by Fair Use of the U.S. Copyright Law, are allowed without written permissions, as long as such quotations do not cause damage to the book's commercial value. For permissions, write to the publisher, whose address is stated below.

Printed in the United States of America.

ISBN   978-1-949746-69-3   (Paperback)
ISBN   978-1-949746-70-9   (Digital)

Lettra Press books may be ordered through booksellers or by contacting:

Lettra Press LLC
18229 E 52nd Ave.
Denver City, CO 80249
1 303 586 1431 | info@lettrapress.com
www.lettrapress.com

THE WHITE HOUSE

WASHINGTON

January 2, 2018

The Reverend Handri Timbuleng
Canal Winchester, Ohio

Dear Reverend Timbuleng,

Thank you for your kind message and prayers. The unwavering faith of the American people has sustained our country through the best and worst of times. As we look ahead, as one Nation, we will fulfill our sacred duty and deliver upon the promise of America for all of our people. We will strengthen our national spirit and ensure that America continues to shine as a beacon of freedom for all the world to see.

Melania and I are heartened by your support. Thank you for taking the time to share your thoughts and for keeping us in your prayers.

God Bless America,

Donald Trump

With best wishes,

Rev. Handri Timbuleng
8782 Creekwood Place
Canal Winchester OH 43110

July 7, 2017

The President
The White House
1600 Pennsylvania Avenue, N.W.
Washington, DC 20500

Dear Mr. President:

I received a message from God that you are the first of three gifts for our country and felt compelled to write a book about this. I wish to honor you by giving you a gift copy of my book and hope you will find it interesting, inspiring and informative.

I have watched with interest your early presidency and am hopeful that through your leadership we may together find a new way that strengthens the life of every person. In these days, may God's blessing and spirit be upon you and guide you.

I hold you in my prayers and hope that God will keep you safe as you serve in this important way in our country's life.

Most respectfully,

Rev. Handri Timbuleng
Pastor, GPDI Columbus Church

"I have known Pastor Handri Timbuleng for a number of years. He brings a passion to all that he does. He has a deep love for God and for people after having suffered much while in his home country of Indonesia."

Pastor Dave Long-Higgins

As a Muslim and an author *"The Ignored Cries of pain and Injustice from Mauritania, 2015*, Stadford Publishing, I have met, worked with and known Mr. Timbuleng couple years ago. We have always discussed and exchanged ideas. I believe that he has a deep faith in humans and their capacity to improve their lives. He has shared with me a lot of his personal experiences that were very amazing. I see him as a man who is very optimistic and courageous. He has a great heart and wants to assist every person in need regardless of their religion, race, and believe or origin. This is how it should be to have peace all over.

His vision is great. It is a change in the way problems should be handled. His vision of life can be unrealistic but but if realized will be beneficial to the whole mankind.

Brother Sidi B. Sene

ACKNOWLEDGMENT / INTRODUCTION

I felt Honored blessed and joyful when I sat down and started writing this book. It was like a privilege for me to have an opportunity to write this book filled with a lot of gifts. God spoke to me about America under Donald J. Trump, the new president elect. After a long fight, finally Donald Trump won. This came like a real gift from God to America. Donald Trump is a Christmas gift to America because he was elected one month before December. He is Christmas although the reason for Christmas is Jesus Christ. This book brings full security for America along with prosperity and confidence. It also brings back hope and faith in American families. It also allows one to read about the greatness of God by him answering the longtime prayers of 265 million Christian believers in the United States. As you may know, as Christians, we have, for years, wore their t shirts with the logo" Pray for America" . We did this every Sunday and even some Saturdays. We went out of the church to the park where so many people were enjoying themselves. Therefore a huge crowd of people in the park see our t shirt with "Pray for America" printed on it. There rise many chances of others to honor, respect and pray for America. This is what the book is all about: the answer of the prays of 265 million Christian believers in the United States. Once again this book is written and loaded with the concerns about the economy in America to change direction. It elaborates on how to cancel the debt, how to overcome the Social Security in 2030 and how to make America great again. I would like to say that we are entering the 4 golden years for believers in this country. These 4 golden years are going to be under the administration of Donald J. Trump, the president elect of United States. The hope of this book is to be the answer of the longtime prayers for America. This book will let you know what is the really answer, what is the really gift that God gives America as an answer to our longtime prayers. One thing I discovered is that God has never answer our prayers. Once again God has never answered our prayers. God always answers above and beyond abundance. This book is about the love of God, the lavish love of God. It is like the reckless love of Abba Father, our God, and our father in heaven. It is like what we see in the story of the prodigal son. We know that the prodigal son comes back after leaving his house. He comes back to his father not because he loves his father (wrong motive) but because of his stomach. He is just hungry. This is not the good reason for the son coming back to his father but still like Abba the father loves his son like the love of God, lavish love of God. The reckless love of the father in heaven who always answered the need of His son abundantly, above all and beyond all expectations (even if the motive is wrong). As the son kept coming back to his house because he was hungry. When, at one occasion, he met his father, the father brought him a robe, put a ring on his finger and slaughtered a cow, a fat animal to honor his son. This is what I would like to express in this book. God did not answer your prayers. He over answered them above and beyond your expectations. As we said, we just prayed God to help America like a son.

We did not think about the love God may bestow on America. We pray to God by just fasting and uttering all types and forms of pray known to ask him to help America overcome the economic and politically situations she is in right now. If you, carefully, read this book, you can see the real over answer of our prayers related in this book. I would like to give 2 reasons why this book is a full authority from Heaven. The first one, you may say this is only Handri Timbuleng writing the book he has in his mind, but what really happened is like when you see a police office in the street and he raises his hand instructs a huge truck trailer to stop. The truck stops because in the palm of police's hand, he has the law although it is not written nor is it visible. The truck has to stop because the police just raised his hand as a sign to stop. Another example: you see a policeman who is short and skinny and may not look like gentleman. He looks much like macho, but we know that behind this police officer there is the law, the order, the rules and regulations that back him up. There is the entire army backing him up, there is the whole marine corps, there is navy and its seals, there is the air force, there is the national guard and you name it, and it is there to back him up. With this entire people behind this little short skinny police, we feel obliged to respect and obey him. This is why when he raises his hand to instruct this driver who has behind him a tractor trailer maybe a triple trailer on the back, he stops. This is the same thing like me, I'm only the writer of this book to tell you about the gift you are about to open. Behind my hand there's a bigger but invisible ones that always lead me into how and what to write. This is the big one behind my little hands. He has an army of angels with fire swords in their hands. They are ready to fulfill what I'm writing down, to make this word, this writing success. We all know that no word from God will fall to the ground. All his words will, always, reach their destination. It is like, the known, smart rocket bombs we use in the Middle East. When these smart rocket bombs are launched, they are not going to hit a target other than what they were programmed for. Therefore when you read the word of this book and believe in them it gives you hope and will make your dream come true. It gives prosperity back to America and will give your confidence as in the psalm 91. You have security and defense not only from the American military, but the military of heaven. This is going to happen and no one will fail in this book. It will become reality. As in Luke 5:5 5: Simon answered and said to Him "Master, we have toiled all night and caught nothing; nevertheless at your" WORD" I WILL LET DOWN THE NET. The second thing I would like to say to you is that when you say that this is reality, so to speak. People will say that this is real life. I would say that it is spiritual life. Spiritual realm is more real than the real life. Once again I would say that spiritual realm is more real than what we call real life because what comes from the spiritual realm is going to be an implementation or a breakthrough. It is going to be the answer of real life. I do encourage the readers to utter a prayer before you start reading this book. It will open your hope to a bigger one. Remain with your faith in in having faith in all works that I have written in this book. This will bring your joy back; bring your dream back of an America with 119 million millionaires. America should have119 million new millionaires and the wiping out of the big debt of America which is about 120 trillion Dollars is going to happen in 2030. Everything has been canceled with the spiritual realm. That's what my message as an acknowledgment and an introduction. I hope you have a happy time and joyful time reading this book over and over again. Do not just read but join in the action. You must have the attitude of action and remember this "God" doesn't need your "plenty". You may have said that" if I have plenty I will serve God". "If I have plenty of this or that, I will follow God. God doesn't need your "plenty". God needs your "availability". The last word I would like to say to you is leaving God with all in your life. God is going to be "God of all or not at all". I repeat God is going to be God of all in good and bad, in health, in sickness, in plenty and in the short, God is the God of all or not at all. When Abraham could still perform and father Ishmael, Abraham call God: "Mighty God" but when Abraham was 100 years old and could no longer performance anymore and was hopeless to have a child, Sarah laughed at him and said" how can I have pleasure? And finally they procreated Isaac and Abraham call God:" All Mighty God"

I am going to close with one story that is a joke. It's a funny story. It was about a young man who was fat. He wanted to go camping and hiking on the mountain. After he almost got to the top of the mountain it became slippery and wet. He started slipping off and going downwards .He luckily reached to a tree branch and hung to it. It was a very dark night. He could not see a thing. This young man was really heavy. Thank God he did not hit the ground. If he ever reached the ground he would die because it was a very high and really steep mountain. So he thanked God and prayed: thank you God. I need your angels to help me get down from this tree; as your provided me with your angels that helped when I was falling from the mountain top. At the end, God sent him a little old and skinny angel. The angel was not only old but it really was skinny and short too. The angel came to him and said:" let me help you". The big fat man refused the offer. He added that it was not possible because the angel was skinny and him fat and big. He wondered how the Angel could help him. The angels said to him:" give me your hand, release the branch and take my hand, you are going to be alright. All this happened in the darkest night. He just refused and then asked: God why did you send me this skinny angel? To make a long story short, he waited and kept refusing the help of the angel. Nevertheless, in the morning he was about 30cm from the ground. He realized that he would be alright holding the angel's hand because he was only 30 cm from the ground. Sometimes we believe in God but we don't trust Him. So this is about how to believe in God. We must not only believe in God but trust him. The other story is about a guy who likes to cross from mountain to mountain. He owns only 1 rope during this trip from the first mountain to other mountain. But the guy is good at playing the circus. When he always played the crowd shouted" we believe, we believe you can do it. The guy was so amazed that he asked:" do you believe that I can make it to the end of the mountain? "The crowd yelled:" yes, we believe you can." There he asked:" is there anybody who wants to hope on my back while I cross to the other end? He is only going to me while I hang on my back while I am walking on the rope to the other of end of this mountain. The crowd suddenly stopped saying we believe, we believe. They stopped saying we believe although they still believed but were not going to say that. There was a little 5 years old kid. He comes up and said" I am going to do that. The guy said "come on young man just hop on my back. He hopped on the back of the guy. Both set off and made it to the other mountain. At the end a reporter came and asked:" I want to get report from this kid". And asked him" why you believe this guy? You knew that there was a risk of falling from the rope while hiking from one end to the other. You could end up dying. You will drop dead on the ground. Why did you do that? The kid answers "he is my dad. That is why I believed in him. God is our father, our dad, he is our Abba father. Just trust Him, do not only believe. Amen.

PREFACE

I would like to open the preface of this book with a story, a true one. I worked for 17 years as a flight attendant and used to fly to Taipei. It is a part of china. While there, I used to go out for dinner. I had a friend. He was a new guy that just got on board. I was at my 4th or 5th years as a flight attendant. My fried has only worked for 1 year. He followed me all the time and everywhere. One night in the middle of a crowd he said: "I want to see a whore. He meant a pleasure woman he can have fun with. Fortunately or unfortunately people in this crowd do not speak English. Most people in china cannot speak English, they speak Chinese. My friend got an idea. With with his left hand he made an "O", and he put one finger inside the "O" and showed to the people in the crowd, the Chinese. They suddenly understood what my friend wanted. They brought us to an apartment in the second floor. We knocked the door and found ourselves with beautiful family. There was a father, a mother, and a 15 years old daughter sitting down and eating. They signaled us to have a seat. After they eat my friend got his transaction done. He paid some money to this family. What all this means is that no matter who you are, rich or poor, you have a financial problem. It does not matter if you are a millionaire or billionaires, you, always, have a financial problem. This is a nasty story. It is awkward. It is a really bad thing that happened with this family because of their financial problem. This is to say that this book is about the finances. If you go to church, 99.99% of the problems are financial or economically. What it means is that our really concern is financial or money. This book is going to be the answer to how we are going to get out of the financial problems. The bad things that happened with the family in Taipei will never happen to you or to us. This was really an unbelievable story that happened in the face of the world. I would like to say that you have to distinguish between a rich man and a wealthy man. A rich man is not wealthy, but a wealthy is always rich. Likewise I say that if you are a doctor and you make 200 thousand dollar a year but at end of the year you spend it all. You have nothing left. Wealthy people have wealth lasts long, up to years in the future. This means that what they made could be enough for all their needs even if they don't work for about 10 years. This is what I call "wealthy". The wealthy have left overs after they satisfy all their needs and wants. The rich people keep working for money using the wealthy people's money making more money and wealth for them. In a nut shell, this is the preface I wanted introducing this book to you. I love to say:" seek the kingdom of God first, and then everything else will be oriented to you by the almighty GOD. It brings me to saying that "Prosperity is not the goal but a product through which we seek God and should find GOD. Amen. God bless you.

I want to talk about an American gift that God spoke to spoke to me about as soon as, Mr. Donald J. Trump was elect president of the United States of America. I was first inspired or it came to me from him as he spoke during his campaign and said that he was going to bring back a "Merry Christmas sign" to every store on every occasion. He promises to just use his power. You know, like helping Christians get back their morality, to this country, especially by discouraging gay and lesbian marriages or even banning them. He also talked about bring the prayer back to schools. What else is he going to use his power? Over democrats and on the Republicans. He is going to use his own power as a president to get Israel back its capital city of Jerusalem instead of Tel Aviv. This, really, is 100 % guard's to Israel.

So this is so amazing. And as a pastor I got inspired by his statement. So he is going to use his power once and he going to use it over the democrats twice. He is going to use his power over the republicans as well to get all the prayers back to their deserved place.

He is then going to cancel all gay and lesbian marriages and make the practice illegal in this country. One other thing he plans to implement: there will be no more "politically wrong language" when we're talking about Christmas. He will enforce the display of "Merry Christmas" banners not happy holidays.

This is a good thing that really inspires me even more. What I would say is that I like to, first and far most thank president elect Donald J. Trump for his faith and obedience. He is going to be the one who gets Christianity back to this country. He is the one who rose above not the others.

So there are a few things God spoke to me about regarding the gift. I would that say the biggest gift that he (God) is going to give us is that of righteousness. This gift of righteousness is clearly laid out, as every believer ought to know, in Roman 5: 17 that said:

"if by the one man's offense death reigned through the one, much more those who receive abundance of grace and of the gift of righteousness will reign in life through the One, Jesus Christ." I, very strongly, believe that before going far that this is the gift that we really need. Some of us may have forgotten that this is the huge. This is the one and real gift. This is the gift that, really, grants one to live, not only on this earth, like the life one is living right in America but to live in heaven live an eternal life. Not a 70 or 80 years life but forever. So the gift of righteousness; this is the gift you receive from Jesus Christ. If you get this gift, I mean gift which means that, this is really 100% free. Sometimes we are confused about the gift of righteousness because we are just doing right not by the righteousness of a gift. The gift of righteousness is like I give somebody a Lamborghini and say this is my gift to you. Just give me $100 a month and you will be fine. This is not a gift even though the Lamborghini costs hundreds of thousands of dollars. He just pays $100. This is going to be a big blessing but not a gift if we have to pay for it. The real gift of righteousness is the one that Jesus gave us by his redemption and what he did on the cross 2000 years ago. So this is the one gift that I want to open up to you guys, to all citizen of America. This is the really gift that cannot be taken away by your mistakes.

Well, come back again, I'm so happy and I'm so joyful and so grateful about this news for America about the restoration of 119 million. New millionaires are going to come to this country.

In 2010 in Meijer super store I just buy something and suddenly God spoke to me to buy a book and that book is "Why we want you to be rich" by Donald J Trump and Robert Kiyosaki.

And now in 2017 God spoke to me what the end of game in Donald J trump Administration.

According this book prediction that the world shape will be change from (like Diamond shape) with wide in the middle and turn to narrow in the middle (hour glass) the old timer clock that people put sand to this bottle and the sand will slowly drop to the bottom because the middle of the bottle is very narrow, so it is telling about the middle class will be going up to rich class or going down to poor class. (No more Middle class).

Finally I asking God how many percent middle class who going to rich class and He answer:, 38% of total population America will move to rich class and I assume that 314 million times 38% is 119 million, so this book try to telling all America citizen be prepare to be MILLIONAIRE and there is 119 million space available !!!

And other reason why I or God want me to write this book is…because the new President wheel is to defend Israel, so God will canceled the future American debt and is about $120 trillion and it will happen in 2030 as the social security Ponze Scheme (all this matter is in my second book with title" The Great I am" with subtitle American Titanic).

Finally this book talking about 3 gift that God Himself presented :

1. President Donald J. Trump. (the first gift)
2. 119 new Millionaire. (the second gift)
3. $120 Trillion future American debt Canceled. (the third gift)

Now what about America National debt ??

The 119 million new millionaire will dealing with that (National debt).

So first of all, I would like to say If you cannot be rich in America you cannot be rich in other country. What I'm saying is if you cannot be rich in this country, you cannot be rich in any other country. So it means that this is the country that gives you a really huge opportunity to be a millionaire. It will be like a piece of cake. One can become a millionaire in seconds. That's why I believe in the businessmen when they keep saying that if one cannot be rich in this country, one will not be able to be rich in any other country. It, really made me joyful and happy to write this book that revolves around president elect Donald J. Trump who is not an ordinary politician, he is a financier and a full size businessman. You know of 119 million millionaires, God chose Donald J. Trump because he is a businessman. He is the one that is going to push 119 million millionaires in the place. As God speak to me that find how many billionaire in this world and after that I find there is 1,826 billionaire of which 48% are Jewish and They are going to help 119 million new millionaire accomplishment as President Donald J Trump Guard Israel. They will lift them up to be a successful millionaire. As I said you got a president that is already a billionaire. It is like He (God) has 119 millions new millionaire in His hands and can do with it whatever He believes fits (what fantastic awesome plan that God has for America shake). Again I would like to give you this encouragement that will get you ready right now that the time has come. The 4 golden years have come. There are things that you have to do and others that you don't have to. I would like to say it as it was first mentioned in the bible "First seek the kingdom of God and after everything else will surround you". What this means is that one will first witness a heavenly economy or God's economy or administered His way. One must first seek the kingdom of God which means that God has to be in the first place. God has always to be in the first place. Never put him in the second or third place, that is to say that he is never second to nobody or anything. He, always, has to be in the first place that's where he belongs, nowhere else. That's God's nature. God must always be in the first place. He cannot be elsewhere. He is God. This is the position that put him above everything and everybody. This not only must be understood by every believer but must be accepted as such. It is not negotiable. Understanding it elevates the believer above those who do not understand it and reject it at the same time. Seek the kingdom of God first which means that prosperity should not be a goal but a result of finding God (PROSPERITY IS NOT THE GOAL BUT BY PRODUCT OF SEEKING GOD). The prosperity is only the reward. That is what believers seeking the kingdom of God receive as their reward. That's only the reward. Reward means the compensation of what you do. Prosperity is not all about, education, experience, relationship with the company or the business that you involved in. All this, really, is only a reward. God will reward one with prosperity. Everything is going to be in God's way. Sometimes if one sees some of the testimonies of a person who wins a business bid, over 100 thousand competitors who have more experience, higher education, better relationship with this project's managers but he suddenly won. He is the one who gets the project although he doesn't have the experience, the education or the good relationship with the company and the people who offer the project. This is why it is called the reward from God. This, no doubt, is going to happen to 119 millions new millionaires that this country counts along others around the globe. So back into the bible, proverb 28:22 says *"a man with an evil eye hastens after riches, and does not consider that poverty will come upon him."*

(IF YOU WANT RUIN SOMEBODY PLAN JUST GIVE THEM TWO FOCUS).

If one does not focus on this one is going to be poor. This is all God's way and will. You need to have one subject of focus one thing: God. You need to focus on him and only him. Do not get distracted by anything or else.... If you are driving a car, you have to focus on the road in front of you. You cannot focus while being distracted by text messaging or talking on the phone. The result is that you will get into an accident. This is the illustration. Another example is that, if you want to ruin somebody's plan or plan to hurt them, get them distracted, prevent them from focusing and they are going be crashed. So don't focus on two things at the same time. Focus on GOD! And you will get to what God has for you. If you want to be successful, you want to get what God has reserved for you. This is to say: Have God first and foremost and you can have everything he has prepared and kept for you. If God can get through you, God can get to you. If you have all the blessings and you live with 100% of your income this is not right. Remember you have to give back the 10%. It belongs to the Giver, GOD. This belongs to him, do not even touch or mess with it. Tithe is only 2 possibilities. With tithe, you give back to God what already belongs to him or you steal it. I would like to introduce to you the phenomenon of the 20/ 80 life. First you have your income or your own money; you have to give 10% tithe to God, and 10% you have to acquire the necessary things like buy insurance, example $1 million Dollar life insurance policy., I don't know how much money you will have to pay for this ($100 to $150 per month maybe). So with this style of life you will make your family a millionaire or even a billionaire one. After you leave this world your children will enter a new life style (they will inherit $2 millions. So always buy a life insurance policy of $1 million. In the future there will always be another millionaire produced from your advice of 80/ 20 (lets say you have 2 kids and they going to inherit $1 million each so came to second generation you will have $4 million and the third generation will have $8 million as assume every kids has 2 kids and so your Idea will make the big family has Asset $16 million). For the 80, you can use it for as you please and for your own sake; but the 10% that belongs to God give it back to him. Use the other 10% to purchase a life insurance policy for your loved ones. With this life style you can live well with a guaranteed inheritance for your family. The bible said that Good a man always leaves a good inheritance for his children. I would like to add to this that life is real easy; what makes it complicated is the lifestyle one chooses to live. Life is very easy especially in America. If you work for a week worth of time, I'm talking about the middle class, the income from that week of work, can provide you with all you need to live for 1 month. So 1 week's earnings can establish your life for 1 month. So the income from the 3 remaining weeks can be deposited in a savings account. But what we see is that the lifestyle is destroying people who are living beyond their earnings. Like whatever you have you always want to drive a Mercedes, you want to get a big house and then you want to eat in the fancy restaurants and that gets you live a crazy life style. In a short period of time you are going to be poor. I just want to give a testimony. It is about a sport man who was a champion and earned millions of Dollars. He did not know how to manage his wealth or lifestyle. From the $5, $10 buffet he jumped to $1000 dinner restaurants. He kept doing it until he realizes that the money was almost gone. He could not refrain from these expensive restaurants. He is slowly slid back to the poverty. He all the sudden went from a millionaire to a poor man because he could not manage his lifestyle. As you can see, lifestyle makes life difficult; Not the life itself, which is very easy and simple. I would also to say that, if you like simplicity, you will not be rich. If you like complexity then you can be rich. So don't like simplicity if you desire to be a billionaire. Like complexity and you could be a billionaire. It is an attitude. If you go away from challenges in which you must stay you could never be a billionaire. If you face a challenge it is supposed to be your opportunity to be a billionaire. If you have ever seen the movie "forest gum", you remember seeing the guy going to sea to make money. He wanted to produce something. At that very the time the weather was very bad and the sea rough. Nobody dared go in. That was a big challenge. He decided to go off shore to fish. In this movie" forest gum" you can see the 2 guys take the challenge that was the opportunity for them to be rich. This is one thing that you have to know. The other thing is always do what you like and not like what you do. I have a friend, who is an entrepreneur, and a devoted businessman. One day this young couple got bankrupt. They got the job working in the entertainment industry sky park operators. So both of them really liked the job. They like the skiing in the winter time which they do greatly, happily, gladly and so on. One day their boss, the owner of the big sky recreation park, asked them to take over the business and make payments back to the owner. They took the offer. Now they are even happier because they like the job and they became successful business people. This is why I want to tell you this; you must do what you like not like what you do. Now it is all about money. All people expect money, a lot of it. I do expect money; you expect money but the wrong thing about is that we don't respect money. We strive for it and when we get it we use it for anything and any way. We buy things we do not need with the money we don't have. We try to impress people who don't even care and then we end up with the big debts of credit cards and store cards and car notes etc. Buying the things that we don't need with the money that we don't have trying to impress people who really don't care is the dumbest thing we do. Let's not do that, please! There is a tip. There is nothing wrong with this. People believe that if we want to be a billionaire we, definitely have be successful. For example you join the army, marine to build a character. This character allows you to learn discipline, to persevere, never give up, this is needed. This spirit of never giving up along a strong character will help you fight with the any challenge. If you serve in the army, the marines, or whatever, body of the security forces and end up going to war or deployed in any unstable zone you foreseeable become affected when you return home. Y spirit records all bad and sometimes horrible things that you witnessed or went through in the battle field. A huge number of these people come back home after the service with bazar syndromes. They enter a struggle with themselves, the families and the societies in which they live. The experiences they had were not joyful and unbearable in life. To overcome these horrible experience, they must be tough people to face life and the take the challenge. They must shine like a star in the fight to become a successful billionaire. There are 2 things that have to be overcome. Being in the military, having experienced horrible things in the battle field, a phase of your life that made of you a tough guy. Nothing wrong. That's good. This is the mentality that prepares a person to be a successful. Besides one has to be smart, have a high IQ which is a blessing from God. It is not given to everybody. When everything is in place, one have to be even smarter, much smarter than ever before. Otherwise after becoming a billionaire one might end up struggling again, lose everything, even file for bankruptcy. This a valid reason one must be smart, embodied in the character of a billionaire to be. The mentality and strength win this type of competition. As said before, one must first seek entry to the kingdom of God. Once entry to the Kingdom is gained, everything else unconditionally comes to you by order of God. There is no need to worry about anything anymore. So you can learn or study from what I explained in this book. Do not worry because when you fight, God will fight for you. When you become successful, you have earned the glory. God has come to you. Do not let people say that you are a good guy. God has been good to you and has modeled your life. Shout out loud that you are safe, you are successful, you are prosperous not because you were good but because God has been good. This does not mean that if you are bad then God is bad. No. Even if you have a bad behavior, God will still safe you. In exchange you must ready yourself for it. This is the attitude that every must believer have in order to be a prosperous person. You are not who others your said you are but who God destined you to be. You are fearfully and wonderfully made. You are a masterpiece. You are the apple of God's eye. You have to believe it. You must be honoring and respectable to God's creation. God create the earth and the skies and whatever is between them including us, the human to whom he gave his own breath and placed us on top of all his creation. We are the masterpiece of God's. We are both fearful and wonderful. The apple of God's eye. So we have the attitude as God has said to Jesus Christ: He is my beloved Son with whom I am well pleased. When Jesus confronted temptation, the devil said that if was the Son of God, he must have do this. The devil always omits word "beloved" (its counter production for devil to tell Beloved son). Therefore one is just not a son but a beloved son. What he is going to give is heaven (God is good not because we are good but God is good because God is Good). He is going to allow us, to redeem it as a reward. He is going to safe us and finally deliver us from evil and from the sin. We, then, must understand that only the righteous man can get to heaven. It is clearly mentioned in Bible that the wealth of the unrighteous man is going to fall into the hands of the righteous one. We are the righteous men, You and I. We are alive because of a righteous God, because. He redeemed us. He did it because the father, son and the Holy Spirit do not want to live in heaven by themselves only. What they really want is to be with you and I. That is only reason why He brought Heaven down on earth to save us. His only purpose is that we can live happily, joyfully and forever. When I preach, I, always say that heaven is really a good place, a nice place, a top of the top place. Everything good and beautiful is in there. But like I said there is no heaven without Jesus. I just choose not to be in heaven without Jesus. This is what we call a relationship. A deep love from God. It does not mean that one loves God. No! This means that God loves one. Talking about love, one can, with certainty state that it is an old, very old phenomenon. It goes back to the Ten Commandments, during the era of Prophet Moses. If one is still alive and abides the laws of the Holly bible One's condemnation should have been death, but the spirit gives and preserves life as advocated in the ministry that is written on the stone. We must understand that we have to love our neighbor, love our God with all your heart, our entire strength and everything. Until now, nobody can follow the Ten Commandments exactly as they are set. Loving your neighbor, then God with all your heart, your strength, your everything has never been done except by one man, Jesus. He has to die because he did it with all. What we do now is you not loving God with all, but we still receive from him wealth, care and health. The New Testament describes it as really love. We do not love God but he loves us and provides for us. Even as sinners God still love us. What attitude in life should we adopt in order to receive God's love? This is a deserving question that must be answered. Our love for God is shaky. It has ups and downs. To answer this very important question, we must explore the story of Peter. It is a very inspiring story. Peter has not only pledge but shown his unconditional love for God. During one meeting with Jesus and the disciples, he said to Jesus, even if all the disciples decide to leave you some day, I will never leave you. I will stay with you until death parts us. That was how Peter expressed his love to God. One day when John, the disciple, whom Jesus loved dearly, laid on Jesus and Jesus blessed, he turned to Peter and said "Assuredly, I say to you that this night, before the rooster crows, you will deny Me three times." and at the end of the story when Jesus was being hang on the cross, when Peter denied him. He did not only deny him but along with God, and added a cursing. That was one very bad thing he did. John was standing at the feet of Jesus who laid on the cross, while Peter who promised eternal and unconditional love to God ended up cursing him and denying God. John received God's love.

Your prosperity, your success, your filthy wealth are already paid for on the cross when Jesus died on it. He absorbed all your curses and sins, condemnations, bad luck, future sins. What Jesus did is not only love but mercy. It shows God's unconditional love for you. When God gave his beloved son to save us, he is being merciful, but when Jesus endured all the punishment to redeem us, God was justifying the sacrifice. When Jesus rose up among the dead and showed the holes in his hands to his disciples at meant that we received all the prosperity and the success necessary for a wonderful life on earth. This is the reason why I say, with certitude, that if someone becomes a filthy rich in America or anywhere else on this earth, it is not a result of their efforts, intelligence or courage, but they found the kingdom of God. His Almighty took over the battle from them; he substituted himself for their suffering, by already having paid for all of it on the cross. Some will tell you t they do not care about Donald J. Trump bring prayer back to schools.t I, like many believers; teach my kids how to pray. It could have been much better if they have it inserted in their curriculum and will have to perform it at school. Some teachers may not be good at prayers, but at least Donald J. Trump brought it back to our schools; that's the bottom line.
A swift look at any billionaire will, somehow, expose a little bit of their lives. You will see that they have been in the military, the paramilitary, in the education system etc.

I understand that so many jobs have never paid right for their sacrifices. But they still gather with family and are proud of what they did. There is a man wearing helmet to defend the ball and has fantastic pay and there is a man wearing helmet to defend this country do not pay right as they sacrifice they life and the future of their family. (OMG) There is nothing wrong with that (I don't want to be rich) and some people of faith leave with almost no money in the pocket and joyfully and gladly serve in the ministry. Some will tell you that money is evil I do not really buy it. I am even 100% sure that it is not true.

What is 100% true is the (love) of money which is the root of evil. But if you have money it is not evil. Many are those who say that I'm the one who always preaches the gospel of prosperity. The idea of a gospel of prosperity is wrong. What I believe is that the gospel can bring or produce prosperity. How can someone say that he is blessed, or God has blessed America if you still cannot afford to pay the rent? The Gospel always talks about good news never bad news. So it is good news that Donald J. Trump was chosen by God to bring this country to prosperity. He is the one who, openly, defends Israel. I got my last gift for you guys; it is the gift of all gifts. People always say that you must give to get or get to give. Neither assertion is right or wrong. If you give to get that means you really expect something. Christianity preaches the idea of getting to give. Whatever you get of it you supposed to give. This gets you blessing. Let say I make @$2,000 monthly and pay out of mortgage, utility, car payment, insurance every month is $2,000; do I have to give out all the

$2,000 to helping somebody else? No. That is not a recommendation of the Bible. You have to do that only if you had more than what is required to cover your basic needs of survival. If you make $3,000 and you paid all your bills and took care of all your responsibilities spending only $2,000.The remaining $1,000 must/suppose to help somebody else. Like I said before if God can get through you, God can get to you. In the future, you may get $1 million a month. Since you are good to live with $2,000. You must be ready to help many other with the extra money, $9,98000. This is going to be the lifestyle of heaven or the kingdom administration. Whatever you have, you should be ready to help others. You are going to be the instrument through which the blessing of God will reach the others. So the standard of prosperity or being rich is not how many cars you have, how many houses you have, how much money you earn every month. The real standard of, wealth and success is measured by how many needy people you helped. The more you assist the richer, wealthier and the more successful you are. You should not help people that God doesn't want you to help because he hates them. Just focus on helping those who are really in need .Help people who struggle to make ends meet. We are going to go deep with a detailed strategy. We have to pay attention to this. So the first one is "give to get", the second one is "get to give" and the third one" is give to give". The later is the one that gives a believer the relationship with God. You must know whatever you have is 100% though you are the one who worked hard for it, putting the required efforts into a project. You still must understand that it a 100% came from God. That is "give to give". God has given you so that in turn you give out to a noble cause For example the Colgate Company; since I (born again Christian) in the 1979 they has given away 95% of its profits to charities, and other good will entities. It survives on 5%. They yet pay the tithe of 10% and grow to 15, 20, 35, up to 95%. This is what I'm call "give to give" Whenever you get to this level, you can be called a really wealthy and filthy rich person. The difference between being rich and being wealthy is that rich people are not always wealthy whereas wealthy people are people always rich. For example, if the salary of doctor for the year is $217,000 a year and he spends all the money within a year, this what is called a rich person (rich people working for their money). But if he can have can spread the money to decently live of it for a period of 10 years without any major financial hardship then this is called a wealthy person (wealthy people makes money working for them).

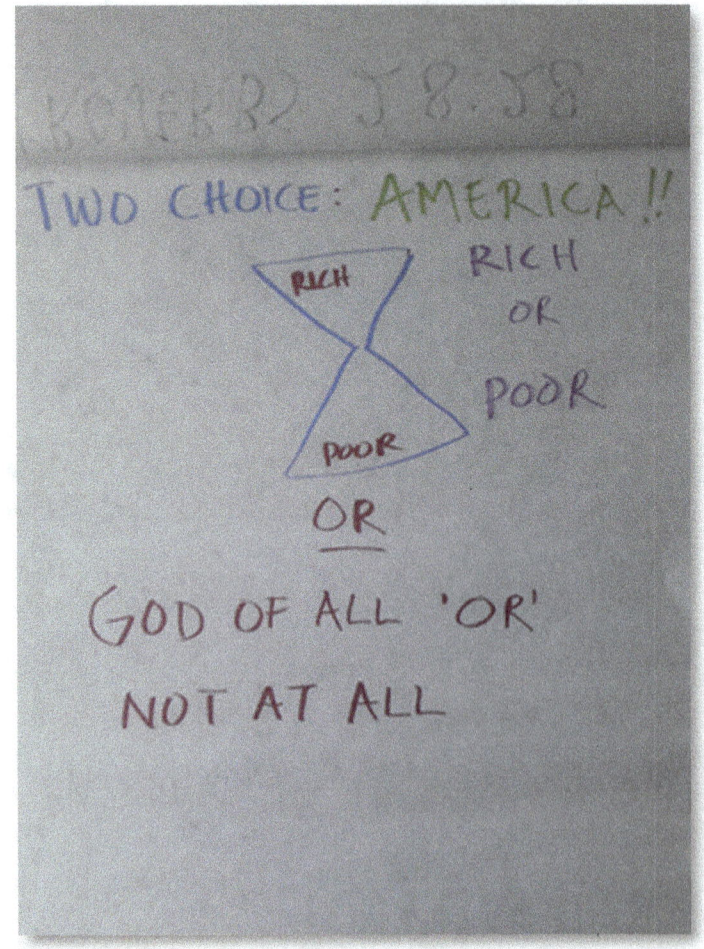

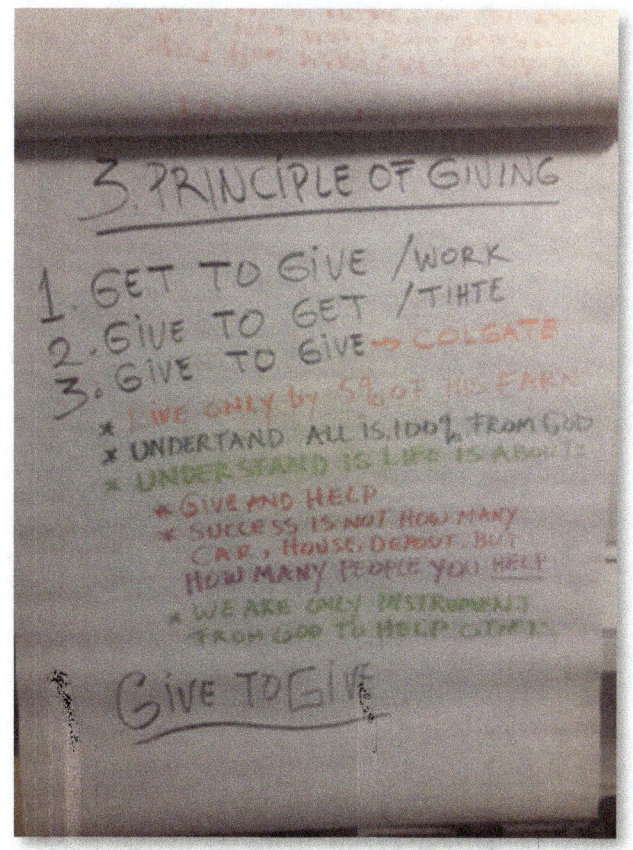

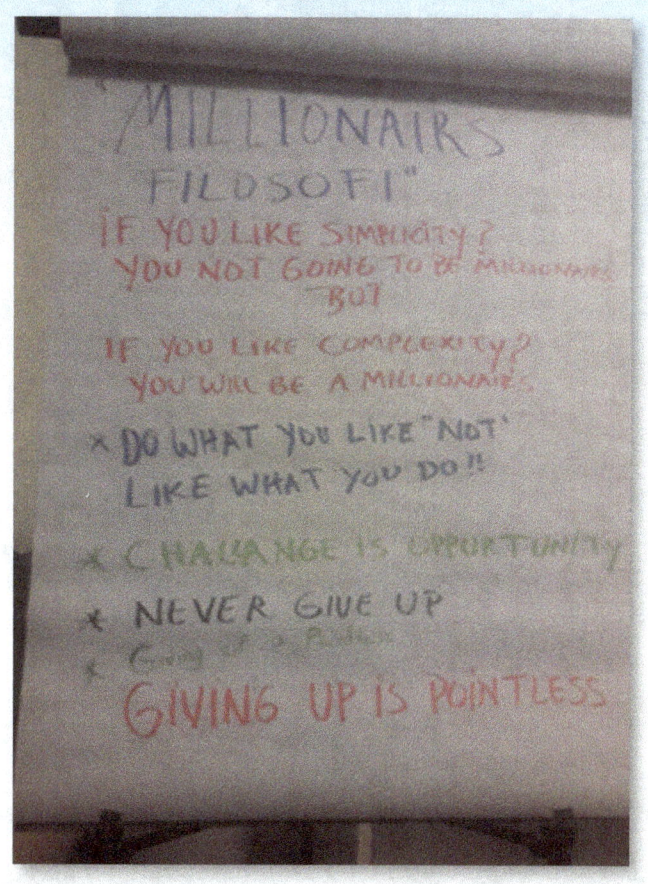

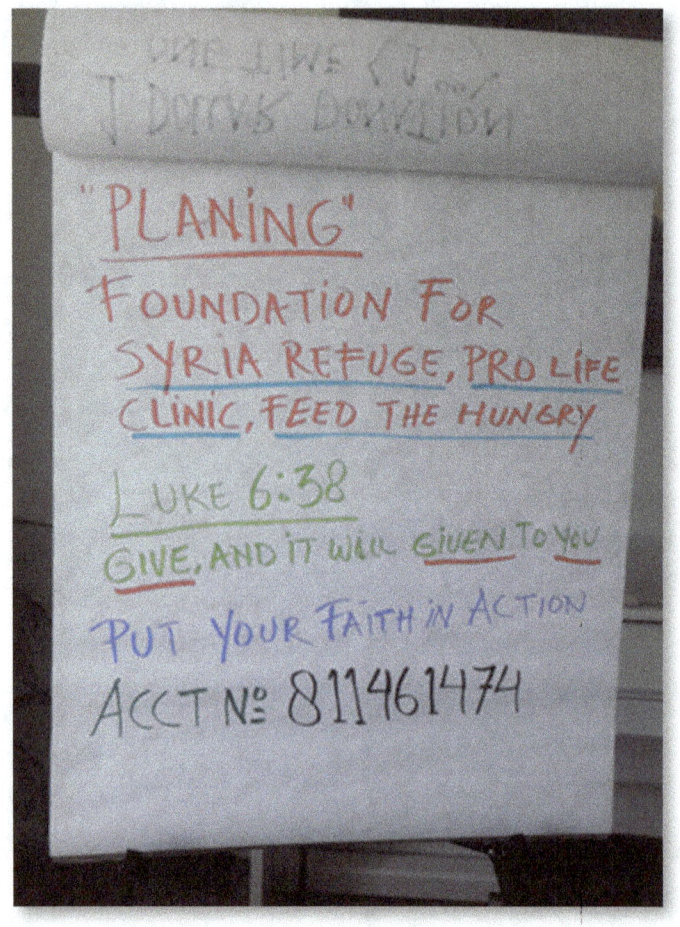

This brings me down to one thing I would like to share with you my brothers and sisters in Jesus. I have a plan to create a foundation to help every refugees, mainly Syrians, the Middle East, fight against human trafficking, drug users and dealers, gang members, and son and so forth. The aim is to bring them to back to the shepherd, Jesus Christ. These are not bad people. They just went off the road and in need of guidance. Once up and running the foundation will need your help with only a onetime $1 gift. If every Christian in America, which are believed to be around 265 million, can help with $1, to assist this mission of putting together a foundation, it will come up to $265 million. Why do I have to sympathize with the refugee because I experienced their fate in the past? This was back in 2001. I came to America, followed all the rules and regulations, and got my paperwork legally processed. As a result I gained legal status. I then could bring my family to live with me. The possibility of bringing my family to America was a joy. But they had to wait for the paperwork to be processed. I was delighted about being able to bring my family from Indonesia as an immigration benefit. They had to go through very lengthy steps of the process. Sometimes in the middle of 2004, God spoke to me about bring my family to United States of America. Everything was going as expected until suddenly the us Embassy in Singapore, where the process was taking place decided to halt everything. The reason was because we were from Indonesia. They said that my family has to start everything from scratch in Indonesia in order to be allowed to come to the US. I had to travel to Singapore to explain to the consular authorities that that it was impossible to re start everything from Indonesia. They still would not agree. My main concern was that I already sold everything back in Indonesia, my house, my car, everything that I owned. The money I received from those sales was being used for my family's stay in Singapore for the 6 months period before they could enter to US. It was a very sad moment of my life. I decide not to give up and was strengthened into this by my faith in God. I started to work 2 jobs in order live and send the money to my family still trapped in Singapore. Since they were going to stay in a hotel for couple month or until the issue is resolved. I couldn't afford to pay my rent in here. I ended up sleeping in my car and taking showers in the rest areas. I was getting skinnier day after day and looked really horrible. I was hammered by the debt collectors because I didn't pay my car note along other credit cards that I had. Sometimes I had to sleep in the rest areas. One day a police officer approached me because he noticed that I was always sleeping in the rest areas. He advises me to go to a motel or a hotel. I could not afford neither. Actually, I seldom, went to the motel. That was only to shower and brush my teeth. I had to work 16 hours shifts for the 2 employers (I has bleeding when going to rest room problem but I don't care). At a given time, I found the shelter refugees. I applied for accommodation and was accepted. The room was a very tiny and I was instructed by the manager not to leave my belongings there because they could be stolen by somebody. I lived in fear and suffering for over 6 months.

Finally one day, directed by God, one of the security personnel working at the embassy decided to help my family by having them speak with the head of security in there. They seized the opportunity and explained the situation in detail. They immediately were issued the letter to travel to the US. But before they really could board a plane come to America, they had to have a medical checkup performed and buy their flight tickets. It was like I was carrying the whole world on my shoulders. It turned out that I was not alone in this struggle. I was very fortunate. The church provided me with money to buy tickets for my wife & my 3 kids, although I had to pay it back so that someone else could profit from it. It was a blessing. To make a long story short, they finally flew to USA. This is the reason why I really would like to help the entire refugees without regard to race, religion or national origin through this foundation, by providing food and shelter while they stay close to their country of origin with the possibility of returning home whenever it fits. I want, with your assistance, create a foundation and name it "God's Samaritans". The idea came from the Samaritan guy who helped somebody who was not even from his family. This Samaritan was not even a Jew. It looked like an enemy has helped them. I would like to start this foundation on the same basis with your assistance. I have always felt that I was not alone in this adventure although I am the only one who is living the dream. Sometimes when I am writing a book I have the feeling that I am alone I always act like wise people and say to myself that I was alone and one but have people around me in the shadow. They helped in every way they could. I knew that I could not do everything by myself but fought with my body and soul to do one thing useful for society. This is why I'm going to put up this foundation regardless of what it could cost. I know that with the will of God and the help of all his children It will prevail. I am fueled and encouraged by this one man who has always supported and encouraged me a pastor in the united church of Christ, Pastor David Long Hagan. This is the man who has helped me with the writing of my books. If I have in my active 3 books that are successes it is thanks to him. He has helped me with everything, from start to end. One day I told him that when I graduate from bible school I will build churches. It is a vision from God he instructed me build 100 churches. He distributed them as follows: 20 in the America, 20 in Europe, 20 in Australia, 20 in New Zealand and 20 in Indonesia. Right after I told him, I added that I already was 54 years old and he replied: so am I. This pastor has already had 20 years' experience of the ministry in the United Church of God. While I was going back and forth I'm talking about writing a book; one day I was meeting with him then we talked about the refugees. Miraculously, I came up with the idea of putting up a foundation aimed at helping refugees. He was thrilled by the idea and in a split of a second, said go for it. That's a good idea, then, you would not have to worry about writing books no more. With that as a starting point along with my personal experience and with my Islamic encounters, I was very well equipped to start working towards the creation of this foundation to help, starting with Syrians, refugees around the globe. Many of whom are persecuted because they are Christians, other because they are minorities but most are children and women caught in war torn zones. They are beheaded, and go through all types of horror while the world sits back and watch. Being silent, not concerned, is encouraging what is happening. I just want us, as a community of the children of God, to help. We can do this and change a lot of lives with a one gift of $1 that is all it takes to make a legacy forever that will stay forever. We are the fortunate ones who must use a fortune to assist the least fortunate. We can eat well, sleep well, have the type of cars we want when elsewhere, our brothers and sisters, go to bed hungry every night, have no clothes, are exposed to harsh and brutal winters, uncertain days and long night with no hope that there will be an end to their nightmare. They cry and cry because they are so desperate. We act like we do not hear their calls for help or see the conditions they are in. While here in the US, we over eat, over drink and over sleep. This is all this book is about. Hopefully we all will be blessed and so will be our beloved country, America the President of United States, Donald J. Trump and his administration. May God bless all the programs that the government will implement in the 4 golden years on behalf of the Christian Community in America and around the world.

Good morning, I just want to share a little bit of my story and how the foundation came up in my mind. It is going to be my main concern right now after I finish writing this book. I worked as a flight attendant, then a flight steward for 17 years. When I graduated from high school in 1980 and in 1982, I joined the Indonesian government airline for almost 11 years. After that I joined a private airline for almost 6 years .The private company ended up filing bankruptcy and went out of business. After the airlines closed I went to a seminary school, Harvest International Theological Seminary in Karawaci, Jakarta, Indonesia. I graduated in 2000. At the preparation of my scrimptions, I got a word from God telling me that I have to build 100 churches of which 20 in America, 20 in Europe, 20 in Australia, 20 in New Zealand and 20 in Indonesia.

Right then a question rose up: believe in it or not to believe in it? Suddenly, a year later, in 2001 I was already in America. After 17 years in America, there was 1 church I build instead of 100. This the reasons why I wrote it down in my scripture as soon as I graduated from the seminary school. It came up in my mind and I always consulted and shared my thoughts with Pastor David Long Hagan. When I matured the idea, I took my time and went to him trying to have an answer. I told him that I, already, was 54 years old had a vision and a mission from God that consisted of building 100 churches. I inquired why not just build 1 before I disappear. I knew Pastor David since 2009. He is a great pastor. I used to openly borrow his church for my congregation. I share his sanctuary from 2010 through 2012. When I had to evacuate I went back to house service. Going back and forth, he told me that we were about the same age. After all I told him that I wanted to write my 4th book, he said, why not. Discuss the ideas with your Moslem friends and ask them to add their ideas and talent to the general idea of your book. After 1 hour of conversation with him, I went back home. On the way back, I was recalling him talking to me about the Syrian refugees and the enormous difficulties they were facing out there. This got me inspired and the idea kept sinking in my mind day after day. In know that God told me that America has the power to win the soul, the heart and the hearts of people in the Middle East.

I will even go further by saying that America has a double power: a military one provided by our troops on the ground and a second one through our resources that we dispose of and that can win a great portion of the Middle East for Christ. So back and forth God is telling me how to use the available resources in order to win the soul, the hearts and minds in the Middle East. The idea popped up to assist the Syrian refugees starting with the most vulnerable ones: the children, the women and the elderly. Using the resources we dispose of we will also help the gang members, street children, the homeless, the drug distributors and users along other human being in difficulties etc. I, immediately, called him, to meet him one more time to share the idea I had. At this second meeting I informed him that I have a desire and God has spoken to me about the power of America. He reiterated the double power it disposes of that could win all of the souls, the hearts and the minds in the Middle East. It might sound controversial since Hillary Clinton promised to bring around fifty five thousand Syrian refugees. The idea drained out more than forty five millions voters of her electorate. These US citizen and potential voters hated the idea of bringing those refugees on US soil. Nothing wrong with their choices. We must respect their choices. They had to use their voices to express their feelings. We are in the greatest democracies out there on the one hand. On the other hand, I see them as a human being amongst which there are a lot of Christians who are stuck in the refugee camps. I talked to him about the foundation's aim to help the refugees and others in need in America and all over the world. Although the foundation will start locally it will reach out to the International community and spread its wing across the globe. I explained that we will NOT bring the refugees to America or move them anywhere else. We will take care of them locally by providing them with food, clothes, medicine, doctors and whatever else they may need and that we can afford. He was delighted with the idea and volunteered to become an advisor for this foundation. I got a doctor join me in this adventure he is a medical doctor I invite a son in law on board, who is a public accountant. I have the support of 3 other Pastors for the foundation and last but not least I gained the contribution of a good friend of mine who happened to be a Moslem, a former ESL teacher and now a court interpreter for the Department of Homeland security, the Department of Justice and the Department of States. He is very knowledgeable in immigration matters and a multi language speaker. God keep telling me that America has power, even, a double power: a military power and the multiple resources it disposes of. We can have a lot of missionaries who will volunteer to help these people instead of fighting them in battle field. So why don't we turn this war and it consequences into peace and love to win the souls, the minds and the hearts of people in Middle East. This how I come up with the idea to ask the American citizens which are about 265 million people, the majority of whom are Christians, to assist with one time donation of $1. We will the proceeds in the foundation's account about and use to get it up and running. If for the foundation, every American Christian citizen can give $1 as a onetime gift, for the love of the Lord, we will raise about $265 million in no time. This is very affordable. It can fit any budge. We very strongly believe that any one who loves humans can participate. A Dollar may seem insignificant but can, in this situation change lives. This is going to jump start this foundation to reach the Middle East and the rest of the world. This is really out of politics and greater than any political issues. We just really need to help right away those in need and have nowhere or none to turn to. The United Nations, although present on the field since day one, has its hands full. We are trying to help with the situation. This is a good reason why I have to meet with the president. God spoke to me 17 years ago. I have not even built 1 church. God spoke to me and said:"use it or lose it". It kept coming to my mind. God repeatedly kept telling me:" use it or lose it".

God has made some people with 1 talent, some with 2 talents and others with 5 talents. If the ones with 5 talents produce 10 other talented ones, the ones with 2 produce 4 others and the ones with 1 talent produce nothing. It is because they put their talent on the ground. What happens here is that God has seen the ones with 5 produce 10 and the ones with 2 produce 4; he therefore, comes very happy. Now God is very upset with the one with 1 talent because he decided to give up and produced anything. So this one time gift of $1, is the golden opportunity for America to assist those in need in the Middle East. I have lived in the biggest Moslem country in the world, Indonesia for about 30 years of my life. So I know a lot about the character of these people. This is why we agreed to put up this foundation, and name it a" Good Samaritan". This is a story in the bible. There was a priest, a very good person who was just passing by and, he got jumped on and beaten so badly by some people. On the other side, there's a guy who did not get on well with them. He was a Samaritan. He just jumped in and helped the one in need. This is going to be the central idea of the foundation. It is a Samaritan. It really gets America a new place in the Middle East. It is going to help American assist disaster affected areas worldwide. It will have an international scope and span. So I am asking you to assist this foundation with one time gift of $1.This will bring about what Pastor David said " stop writing book. I will have enough time to focus on the foundation and spreading the word of God. He spoke to me before the second meeting I had with Pastor David. I mentioned to him that I have not even built 1 church and now you are asking me to put up a foundation. God said that this was the way. This is an open door through which you will get to build 100 churches. This foundation is going to be worldwide. Go ahead and aim at building the 100 churches as the foundation grows. You can start building churches in the way you plant seeds. The first one planted will give birth to the others. We live under the same sky, eat the same food, why can't we share the prosperity? I would like us to color the Middle East and America with $1. While staying outside politics and political agendas. This is really an investment in God helping people without regard to color, religion, gender, age or national origin. No matter if I they are our enemies or our friends, no matter if we like them or we don't. As a Christians we are called to love. Because love is unconditional. Jesus said love your neigh neighbors. I hope this to be the good reason to invest in this account by helping people around the world. This is the philosophy I brought with me from my native Indonesia to America. When I arrived in America, I said to myself" Handrie are only one but the other voice says" yes are only one and still one that cannot do everything alone with this work in Middle East. I can do everything to help and speak to others to make it not on happen but better, rebuild a relationship of mutual trust, love and respect between America and the Middle East. The voice kept saying" you can do one thing" This is why I said that I'm only one but I'm still one. I cannot do everything but I can do one thing. I will stop to one thing. Amin, Hallelujah and God bless you all.

Now I'm going to talk about the closing word. So, this is about Psalm 91 & Isaiah 60. We entering the evil times, the bible me mentioned the fact that human beings should love themselves, be proud, never disobedience to parents. They must have regard and respect for authority. They must not abuse of their authority over their families. There is nothing more honest than the Word. The Bible told us that when the world gets darker and darker, the churches are going to get brighter and brighter and more and more revelation will fall into the churches along with the glory of the Lord shining upon the churches. And to the churches and the believers" let us stand and stand up on our feet now". Y'all know that God was confirming the sign and wonder. So you know that God is in the house, God know the future, God doesn't wants your heart to be troubled. He doesn't want you to be in fear. The Jewish Rabbi, I learn this from, John J. Lag, is a great man of God., he quoted from the word that if one reads Psalm 91, 7 times, faith will be in the their heart. Jewish Rabbi recommends that people seek to recite Psalm 91 again and again and again. The Jewish Rabbi tells us that in the Hebrew legend tell there's a cloud, little and thick. They called "Little cloud". As we all know there are seeds in the English Bible but clouds in the Hebrew Bible. About the Psalm and the book of psalm 91 has the most Shayin. What is shayin? Shayin is the picture of the sword. You know the letter from Psalm 91. So the Jewish Rabbi said it's the sword that will take the power of darkness away from your life. And they did not know about it. They lived for hundreds of years and never knew that the world, increasingly, became an evil place that was getting darker and darker. I, then, want to do, what I wanted to do. However I want to do it with the participation of my fellow Christian brothers and sisters. You don't tell me what I have to do, when I have to do it and how I have do it. So we are living in that world today. We are near the most important phase of our lives. God said" I don't care about how you raise your family as long as raise them in the way of the Lord. As Joshua said" for me and my house we will serve the Lord". Can I have a good Amen? We are in perilous times. We're in the days where men love other men. But I will speak for all of you tonight, together, in one voice and one heart. Whatever it is that you are watching or doing let's quote Psalm 91, and I believe that God will release the anointing, and that will cover you and your loved ones, your families Amen, for the days to come. We will in the days to come step into John 17 .HE prays the father in the highest priest prayer, the night that he was betrayed and delivered to the hands of the Romans. He pronounced his prayer as follows:" Father I pray to you not only to take them out of the world but then you protect them from the evil in the world, Amen". That prayer was answered for sure. Let's line ourselves to the prayer. Are you ready, all together now one heart one voice read, *He who dwells in the secret place of the Most High Shall abide under the shadow of the Almighty*

*2 I will say of the Lord, "He is my refuge and my fortress;
My God, in Him I will trust." 3 Surely He shall deliver you from the snare of the fowler[a] and from the perilous pestilence.*

4 He shall cover you with His feathers, And under His wings you shall take refuge; His truth shall be your shield and buckler.

5 You shall not be afraid of the terror by night, Nor of the arrow that flies by day

6 Nor of the pestilence that walks in darkness, Nor of the destruction that lays waste at noonday.

*7 A thousand may fall at your side,
And ten thousand at your right hand;
But it shall not come near you.*

*8 Only with your eyes shall you look,
And see the reward of the wicked.*

*9 Because you have made the Lord, who is my refuge,
Even the Most High, your dwelling place,*

*10 No evil shall befall you,
Nor shall any plague come near your dwelling;*

*11 For He shall give His angels charge over you,
To keep you in all your ways.*

¹² In their hands they shall bear you up,
Lest you dash your foot against a stone.

¹³ You shall tread upon the lion and the cobra,
The young lion and the serpent you shall trample underfoot.

¹⁴ "Because he has set his love upon Me, therefore I will deliver him;
I will set him on high, because he has known My name.

¹⁵ He shall call upon Me, and I will answer him;
I will be with him in trouble;
I will deliver him and honor him.

¹⁶ With long life I will satisfy him,
And show him My salvation." Amen. Praise the Lord.

What a beautiful psalm, what a powerful psalm. I'm telling you that this place is charged, that place is watching right know, you can sense it. It's a most tangible powerful anointing, hallelujah. Psalm 91 is a Psalm that God gave for times that we are in, it covered all kinds of evil in the world. If you look at the verse 3, tells us *3 Surely He shall deliver you from the snare of the follower [a], and from the perilous pestilence.* You know the fowler is a bird trap. The devil traps people, he does come and say look on the devil, he will tells you there's nothing wrong when you looking at your star, and the horoscope, there's nothing wrong when playing with the ouiji board, there's nothing wrong doing that kinds of thing, there's nothing wrong watching a horror movie. On the verse 5 and 6, *⁵ You shall not be afraid of the terror by night, Nor of the arrow that flies by day,*

⁶ Nor of the pestilence that walks in darkness, Nor of the destruction that lays waste at noonday.

Watch the word by the arrow that flies by day, God is referring to a piece of stick, but the missile that can travel 7,000 miles (11,300 km) as our globe diameter is only 3,958 miles (6,371 km) that's concerning worry. We are not be afraid because the bible says God promise He will protect us. Amen. So let's see at the 3 category; we have the terror, what the world we living right now is a world of terror now. Imagine our children living in the world that for rush, we were walking down the street we can actually go to the airport in time pass and we were worry about so many things, even take off our shoes, and now all kinds of things, you have to make sure that your I phone is really working, or your computer is working. So the next one is the arrow that flies, the pestilence that walks in darkness, the disease that walks in the darkness, people just thing that we were exercise every day, they run every day so there's a disease that has walking in the darkness in his body. No one detector it, he dropped it. Whatever they said, genetic or whatever God said, there's protection for it. This is Holy Scriptures we have the destruction that is generally covered every day, destruction that waste the noonday, so all of the category of evil you can imagine they can come upon the world because people be afraid they all said in Psalm 91. And for which time, is this seasonal it has certain time? No, verse 5 says by night by day, verse 6, darkness and noonday. In other words it has 24 hours protection. Are you listening, people? 24 hours protection, you must establish this they are people who don't believe that God is not running the world completely. I'm telling you church, God is running his people, his kingdom and his people that in the kingdom, but the people in the kingdom are not willing to follow him, they are still on their own. God is not running this world. If God is running this world, there're be no hospital, there be no default, wars and weapons. Once upon the time God was running this world and there's not a disease, there's no sickness, there's no poverty and there's no death in the Garden of Eden. And then man sin. Bible said the earth that God's given to the children of man. And God is not like kind of giver like a man, if you say, ok give it back to me. No, when God gives, it is given. He is a man that committed high reason, outlaws spirit Satan, but He is a man that will take it back from Satan, from the second Adam, his name is Jesus Christ. And He went back for us. Hallelujah. Amen. He conquered death, the ultimate enemy and rules from his authority and He is alive today. You and I accept the risen savior. Amen

So, this is I want to said to all of us, citizen, believer that 265 million believer in America, let's stop to read Isaiah 60 before we sleep in the night and we see all this scripture on Isaiah 60, how God is going to bless us, how God is going to deliver the wealth in this world to us as a believer, as the righteous, the unrighteous wealth is going to be delivered or transferred to the righteous and then we are not righteous because we doing right but we righteous because we are in Jesus Christ that Jesus give us the gift of righteousness. So we are right because the blood of Jesus. So we read this at night and then in the morning before you going to work, you do activity in the morning, and apply Psalm 91 verse 1 to 22 and you going to go to work. And then in this book I give you like a name card, there is about 911, this phone 911, but actually is not phone 911 to emergency call, but this is Psalm 911. So you going to put this card in your wallet and then there is a account number for our foundation, The Good Samaritan International Foundation, the account and you going to give $1 one time gift forever. So we can work together as everyday you can give for this foundation to reach the people in the Syrian refugee, a human trafficking, a disaster, a drug dealer, you named it, the gang people on the street, and then specially I wanna tell you there's so many people desperate, maybe they are in the disaster made by refugee, camp and they already give up about their life. But still deep in their heart they have hope and in the hope they gonna ask the question like this: if there's a god why I cannot eat well today, if there's a god why I cannot get my medicine, if there's a God why all the people around the world molest their daughters, and if there's a God why he treats me like this. If there's a God, you know that you are the answered with $1. You are the answer that God exists, you are the hands of God, help them, land a hand to the people who are really desperate, people who are being trafficked, people who are lost, help the neighbors who are affected by disaster. They prayed and kept praying. They are about to give up. Why is disaster on, my way? They lost entire families and neighborhood to disaster. Why if there's a God why I don't have my house right now, my clothes, everything I had was wiped out by the tsunami. A lot of things happen to me. Where's God. Why didn't he help me. So once again you are the one who is g hoeing to help them. You are the one who is going to be the answer to all their questions and worries. You are going to confirm the little deep hope that they had to, one day, be answered by God through us. Thank you everybody who read this manuscript and answered the call of a divinely cause. May God bless you and may God bless America. Hallelujah. Amen.

DONALD J. TRUMP

Handri Timbuleng
8782 Creekwood Place
Canal Winchester, OH 43110-9804

142487-83480

AUTO

142487-83480

Certificate of Nomination

This is to Certify that

Handri Timbuleng

Is hereby officially nominated to join as a member
of the
Trump Make America Great Again Committee's
Team 2020
From Ohio
With all rights and privileges granted
Immediately pending receipt of the enclosed
Membership Acceptance form.

Approved by:

Donald J. Trump
President of the United States
January 2, 2019

TRUMP TEAM 2020

Attested by:

Brad Parscale
Campaign Manager, Trump 2020
January 2, 2019

www.ingramcontent.com/pod-product-compliance
Lightning Source LLC
Chambersburg PA
CBHW080024130526
44591CB00036B/2636